16.99

Lonely Planet

50

Natural Wonders

TO BLOW YOUR MIND

Contents

Introduction

Modern life is a rich and varied confluence of information, technology, social interaction, work, travel, family and fun – if you're lucky. There are smartphones in the most remote corners of our world and we have advanced in scientific endeavour further than ever before. Our cities are huge bustling metropolises and they're growing larger every day. More than half of the earth's population lives in these urban centres and this percentage is steadily increasing. However, despite this cumulative urbanisation, there is a tacit understanding among the human race that connection to nature is an essential factor in our happiness.

For all our obsession with man-made wonders nothing compares to the creations of Mother Nature. Vast underground cave systems, wild desert landscapes, breathtaking waterfalls, staggering geology and spectacular vestiges of our prehistoric past all remind us of our small place in earth's story.

And even with our ever-expanding knowledge of the way the world came to be, some landscapes still leave us utterly perplexed. This is the mystery and the majesty of the natural world. In this book we've attempted to capture just a fraction of what it has to offer, and we hope it inspires you to get out and find your own slice of pleasure in the great outdoors.

Beach idyll

Beach of the Cathedrals, Spain

A RELIGIOUS EXPERIENCE THEN?

Some might feel a kind of mystical wonder come over them. Others will marvel at the power of nature – these ocean-side rock formations have been carved by wind, rain and sea for a few years now. And by 'a few', we mean millennia...

I'M FEELING A LITTLE INSIGNIFICANT AGAIN...

Understandable: a human life doesn't scale well to geological time, but go with the flow and bask in the glow of these astounding formations. The naves formed into the 30m cliffs are breathtaking and you can spend hours wandering in and around them.

TIME AND TIDE?

Good question! So: time – go see them while you can. Erosion waits for no woman. Or man. Or rock. Some of these arches will fall into the sea soon enough (geologically speaking). Also – yep, low tide – at high tide you won't be doing much exploring. Time your run well.

GOD, THAT WATER LOOKS DELICIOUS!

Maybe it's divine intervention, but yes, you're right, the water here looks more like the clear turquoise stuff of a tropical beach wonderland, yet here it is in little old Spain. It's a marvel.

Hidden Beach, Marieta Islands, Mexico

SHHH, DON'T TELL ANYONE ELSE ABOUT THIS PLACE! WE WANT IT TO OURSELVES.

The secluded setting of this gorgeous beach is the stuff of wild and romantic fantasies, which is why it has also earned itself the title of *playa del amor* or lovers' beach. Lovesick dreamers the world over have longed to have these golden sands, gently lapped by crystal blue waters, all to themselves, and due to the beach's remote and concealed location there's a good chance these dreams could come true.

HOW DO WE GET IN THERE?

This secret swimming hole, visible from above through dense jungle and cavernous limestone, can only be accessed by swimming or kayaking through a long tunnel of water that links the beach to the Pacific Ocean.

HOW DID THIS NATURAL WONDER COME TO BE?

Mother Nature can't take all the credit for this one. It is believed that military bomb tests conducted by the Mexican government in the 1900s created a whole series of craters, caverns and unusual rock formations throughout the Marieta Islands, one of which being the magnificent Hidden Beach.

50

Moeraki Boulders, South Island, New Zealand

WE IMAGINE THIS IS WHAT IT WOULD LOOK LIKE IF GIANTS HAD ABANDONED A GAME OF PREHISTORIC BOWLS HERE ON THE BEACH.

It does seem implausible, if not impossible, for these strange stone spheres to have been organically crafted, so giants playing beach bowls kinda makes sense. Though, for the less magically-minded, the story goes that the boulders began forming on the ancient seabed in marine mud, created in a spherical shape by calcium diffusion, and were then exposed through erosion over hundreds of thousands of years. Geological studies estimate some of the larger boulders to be over five million years old.

MAGIC OR NO MAGIC, THIS WINDSWEPT COASTLINE IS A CRAZY PLAYGROUND.

It's bags of fun to clamber over the gigantic stone balls, some of which are a huge two metres in diameter, and some sit in clusters, partially submerged in the water.

WE'VE NEVER SEEN ANYTHING LIKE IT.

The boulders are actually not unique to the South Island; the North Island has its own stone wonders known as the Katiki Boulders, and similar spheres have even been discovered in Barbados and parts of North America.

Palawan Island, The Philippines

AHH, NOW WE'RE TALKING – A TROPICAL PARADISE.

The Palawan Archipelago is one of the only tropical wonderlands left in the world that can truly claim the title 'unspoilt', and the island of Palawan sits like a giant shining jewel in the centre of this glittering paradise.

WE'RE HAPPY TO KICK BACK HERE ON THESE WHITE SAND BEACHES FOREVER.

If, however, sunbathing in nirvana starts to get old, Palawan has plenty more to offer of a more active nature.

YOU MAY AS WELL TELL US ABOUT IT THEN WHILE WE FLOAT IN THE GENTLE TURQUOISE WATERS.

Let's see if we can't tempt you into action. There's scuba diving among the numerous WWII shipwrecks at Coron Bay, or snorkelling in the stunning big and small lagoons ringed with dramatic limestone cliffs at El Nido. And the *pièce de résistance*? The Puerto Princesa Underground River. The 8.2km-long subterranean river system is believed to be the longest navigable underground river in the world; it flows beneath a mountain range and empties directly into the South China Sea. Don't miss the opportunity to hire a kayak and explore this uniquely stunning natural wonder.

Santorini, Cyclades Islands, Greece

THE GREEK ISLANDS ATTRACT A LOT OF TRAVELLERS IN PEAK SEASON...
Among the hustle and bustle that takes over Santorini and the other Greek islands during peak season, it's easy to forget the astonishing way these places were formed and the rugged gorgeousness beneath the buildings; but look out over the azure ocean and along the steep cliff-faces and you'll see that this is one of the most lovely places on earth.

THE PEOPLE OF SANTORINI (OR THIRA AS IT IS ALSO KNOWN) SURE KNOW HOW TO MAKE THE MOST OF WHAT THEY'VE GOT.
The traditional Cycladic whitewashing of the buildings that cling to the craggy cliff-faces create such a stark contrast with the sharp blue of the sunken oceanic caldera below that the image has become one synonymous with Greece.

WHO WOULDN'T WANT TO PUT THEMSELVES IN SUCH AN ICONIC SCENE?
Throw in a balmy Mediterranean climate and a sunset that produces an everyday light show of soft red, orange, peach and ochre reflecting off the white edifices, and you have the makings of one of the world's most magnificent sights.

Vaadhoo Island, Maldives

WHAT'S SO WONDERFUL ABOUT THIS MALDIVES ISLAND? THEY ALL LOOK AMAZING!

The Maldives is your go-to place for beach paradise, no doubt. But Vaadhoo takes it up a notch.

COCKTAILS?

The magic does indeed begin after dark, but the bar involved is made of sand. Head to the Glowing Beach (maybe the name gives it away). On a still night, you'll see the dark waters of the Indian Ocean and just the occasional spark of light in the ripples.

WELL THIS SOUNDS LOVELY ENOUGH.

It's only just begun! Where were we? Right... ripples, sparks of light... so, enter the ocean and you'll notice more distinct flashes of light around your ankles. Kick a little water and an arc of blue light, like plasma, shoots out from the ocean.

WHAT ON EARTH ARE YOU TALKING ABOUT?

I'm setting the scene. What we have here is bioluminescent plankton that reacts with oxygen and generates a glowing blue light. These critters have made a home here and the effect is mesmerising. Try cupping the water in your hands; it sparkles then fades to black – then you shake it in your hands to get a handful of molten blue fire. Natural wonders just got interactive!

Deep down

Cave of Crystals, Mexico

IS THIS TRICK PHOTOGRAPHY?

It is 100% the real deal – it's like you've stumbled upon the Land of the Giants. No one has seen bigger crystals than these. In fact, not many people have seen these at all, for that matter!

WHERE IS THIS FANTASY LAND?

Head to Mexico if you're not already there. Then to Chihuahua, from where you can make your way to the mining town of Naica. Once there, you'll find out you can't actually visit the cave.

ARE YOU MESSING WITH ME?

Look, this is a natural wonder of the first order – it would be insane not to include it. But at this point in time, unless you're a researcher or a miner, it's unlikely you'll be getting down there.

DOWN THERE?

It's 300m below the surface and the heat, due to the chamber's location above a lava flow, is so great that you can only bear 15 minutes marvelling at the crystalline structures before heat exhaustion becomes a threat. But a cave filled with selenite crystals that can be metres long and wide, weighing tens of tonnes, is impossible to ignore. Just knowing it's there makes us feel pretty excited.

Darvaza Crater, Turkmenistan

WE'RE KEEPING OUR DISTANCE FROM THIS ONE.

Despite the furious and fiery appearance of this dramatic opening in the earth's crust, which also has the less inviting monikers of the 'Door to Hell' and the 'Crater of Fire', it's actually possible to walk right up to the edge and peer over into the abyss.

WE'LL TAKE YOUR WORD FOR IT.

Believe it or not, the flames inside the crater actually make it safer for travellers to get up close to the gates of hell. The depression was initially created when a huge chunk of earth collapsed into an underground cavern on a natural gas field. In 1971, geologists set the crater on fire in order to prevent the spread of dangerous methane gas reaching local communities and it has been burning continuously ever since.

IT LOOKS LIKE IT'S EVEN POSSIBLE TO CAMP ON SITE.

Tour groups will pitch tents for travellers just a couple of hundred metres from the edge where, at night, the flames flicker mysteriously, tempting you over to journey to the centre of the world.

Grand Prismatic Spring, Yellowstone National Park, USA

CONVINCE US THESE COLOURS HAVEN'T BEEN PHOTOSHOPPED.

Don't press us on the scientific details, but as far as we know the striking prismatic colours of this, the world's third largest hot spring, are created by bacteria. Not as romantic as it looks, right? At the centre of the spring, the temperature is too hot to sustain any life so you get the clear blue tones, but as the water cools and spreads, different photosensitive bacteria move in and create the different colours.

WHATEVER THE REASON, IT'S A BRILLIANT SIGHT.

The huge spring is over 110m across and 40m deep and with its kaleidoscopic colours, constantly bubbling surface and swirling steam it makes a serious play for top sight in the magnificent Yellowstone National Park.

IS THIS LIKE SOOTHING HOT SPRING TERRITORY – AS IN, CAN WE GET IN?

Are you crazy? Did you not hear the bit we said about 'too hot to sustain life'? Even if you weren't to heed our warning, getting close to the colourful parts of the springs is a no-no. Please stick to the wooden paths.

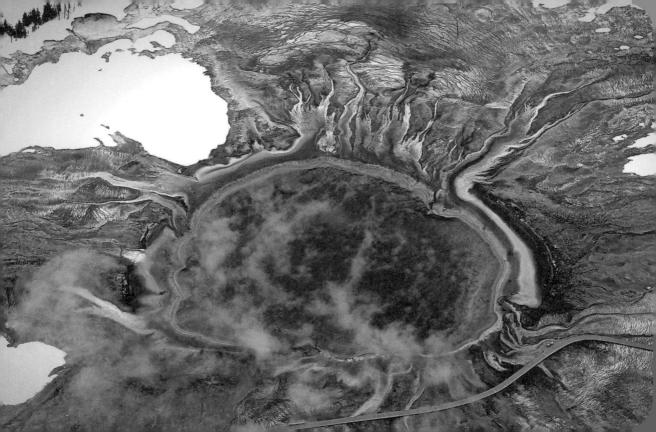

The Great Barrier Reef, Queensland, Australia

THE SETTING FOR THIS NATURAL WONDER IS PRETTY WONDERFUL IN ITSELF.

As your boat sails from the golden sand beaches of Northern Queensland across the expanse of crystal blue waters you might think the scenery spectacular, but that's nothing compared to what you're about to see below the surface.

WHAT UNDERSEA MAGIC ARE WE IN STORE FOR?

The staggering statistics tell a story in themselves – this is the world's largest single structure made from living organisms; so huge, in fact, that it can be detected from space. It is made up of over 2900 reefs and 900 islands that stretch for over 2300km. But all you'll really notice, once you dive down, is the rainbow of marine life that crowds around you. It's a tropical fish play centre with sharks, stingrays, sea turtles and even the elusive and enigmatic dugong thrown in for good measure.

IT'S TRULY AMAZING, BUT AREN'T WE IN DANGER OF LOSING THIS UNIQUE SITE?

Global warming and the resulting rise in temperature of the earth's oceans has caused widespread bleaching of the rare coral, thus destroying the essential habitat of the reef's marine life. The reef needs its environmental warriors as well as its tourist trade to ensure its survival.

Great Blue Hole, Belize

FLIPPERS – CHECK. GOGGLES – CHECK. I'M READY.

Optimist – check. At a depth of 125m, you're going to need a little more gear than that to explore this oceanic vertical cave.

I THOUGHT IT WAS A HOLE.

Well, whatever you want to call it, it was formed tens of thousands of years ago by glaciers – and it wasn't always filled with seawater. If you get your scuba gear on, you'll see the stalactites that most of us associate with caves.

NO NEED TO GET SNOOTY. ARE YOU SURE I CAN'T JUST SNORKEL?

You can, actually. Just take a boat for a day trip out to the hole. You can swim around the hole's edge and get a feel for this crazily beautiful place. But it's with diving gear that the full majesty of this heritage-listed site comes to life. The water is famously clear – gin-clear as they say – and sea life abounds.

HOW'S THE FISHING?

None of that, thank you very much! But if you're after sealife snapshots, reef sharks, angel fish, and parrotfish ought to come into frame. As a cave, it's not a rich, colourful undersea wonder, but as a fish tank, you're going to have plenty to see.

Hang Son Doong, Vietnam

SO WE'RE OFF FOR SOME SPELUNKING?
Not just any caving adventure – this is a journey through the world's biggest cave. Discovered in 1991, the magnificent cavern soars to over 200m in height, 150m in width, and stretches for a jaw-dropping five kilometres in length. It is so expansive that it contains its own ecosystem, complete with jungle, river, lake and temperature zone.

ALL RIGHT THEN, LET'S GET IN THERE.
Here comes the difficult bit. Hang Son Doong can only be visited on a tour which requires a day and a half trek before you even reach the cave entrance. Once there you need to abseil close to 80m down a rough mountainside to get your first glimpse inside.

DESPITE THE HARD GRAFT TO GET HERE, IT LOOKS LIKE IT'S WORTH IT.
From the moment you see the swirling mist rising dramatically from the cave's entry you know you're in for an other-worldly treat. Once inside, the majesty of this hidden wonder is revealed. Giant limestone karsts form gnarly sculptures that tower over the crystal blue waters of the internal lake, and beams of light from above strike jungle vines and stalactites that stretch for kilometres into the depths of the cave.

Jeita Grotto, Keserwan, Lebanon

OOH, WE LOVE A GOOD SECRET GROTTO.
Despite the discovery of the remnants of an ancient foundry in a nearby cave that suggests the area may have been used for the production of swords thousands of years ago, the modern uncovering of the grotto is attributed to an American missionary, Reverend William Thomson, in 1836. Since then, many expeditions have ventured into the cave and established that it stretches for nearly nine kilometres over two levels.

WOW, IT'S HUGE.
It's actually a system of two interconnecting limestone caverns which provide the escape route for an underground river. This river goes on to deliver more than a million Lebanese with fresh drinking water. Gob-smacked tourists are chartered into the lower section of the cave by boat, but it's possible to walk along the upper galleries under your own steam.

SO INSIDE IT'S THE USUAL ROLL CALL OF CAVE FORMATIONS?
There are stalagmites, stalactites, columns, curtains, ponds and draperies galore, and you'll also see two chambers on the upper level that are distinctly coloured; one red and one white. The colours are created by a chemical reaction at different temperatures. Inside the white chamber is the world's largest stalactite, at a huge 8.2m long.

Lake Baikal, Siberia, Russia

WATER, AS FAR AS THE EYE CAN SEE.
This is one for the record books. Lake Baikal, the world's largest freshwater lake (by volume), stretches out for hundreds and hundreds of kilometres across remote Siberian wilderness, 636km in length and 79km in width, to be exact. The lake's statistics are extraordinary: it contains roughly 20 per cent of the world's unfrozen surface fresh water; more water than all of the Great Lakes in North America; it plunges to a world-beating depth of 1642m; and is also considered the world's oldest lake, at around 25 million years of age.

THE WATER LOOKS CRYSTAL CLEAR BUT A LITTLE ON THE CHILLY SIDE.
Although winter temperatures in the lake drop to nearly -20°C and the whole thing gets covered in a thick blanket of ice, the summer sees a warmer side emerge and hordes of tourists descend to splash around in the pristine, and rumoured life-extending, water.

WE STILL THINK IT'S TOO COLD TO TAKE OFF OUR CLOTHES.
Then consider taking a hike around parts of the perimeter. A walk to the top of the Svyatov Nos peninsular gives you stunning 360° views of the lake and surrounds.

JEJU CITY, JEJU, SOUTH KOREA

Manjanggul Lava Tube, South Korea

WE'VE HEARD ABOUT LIMESTONE, GYPSUM, DOLOMITE, AND EVEN ICE, MARBLE AND SALT CAVES, BUT LAVA? THAT'S A NEW ONE.

What was once an escape route for basaltic lava from the Geomunoreum volcano, which erupted around 3000 years ago, is now a warren of tunnels and caves that feel like roads to the centre of the earth.

IS IT SAFE TO GO IN AND EXPLORE?

Many of the lava tunnels are open to adventurous travellers, the largest of these being the Manjanggul lava tube. This cavern is nearly 9km in length and in parts is up to 30m high and 23m wide. The interior of the enormous tube is adorned with lava stalactites, stalagmites and other lava formations like helictites, shelves and bridges. The walls are covered in colourful carbonate markings and cave corals, and at the end of one of the passageways you'll see the world's largest lava column at 7.6m.

DID WE JUST SEE SOMETHING MOVE IN THERE?

It's not just tourists who are attracted to the wonder of the lava tube. It's believed that up to 30,000 bent-wing bats call the cave home. That's the largest colony of bats in South Korea.

FRANSTD © GETTY IMAGES/ISTOCKPHOTO

Marble Caves, Chile and Argentina

CAVES CARVED FROM MARBLE? WE'RE LOST FOR WORDS.

As enigmatically beautiful as they sound, these swirling, sculptural spaces have been created by the gentle waves from the glacial Lake General Carrera lapping against a calcium carbonate peninsula over the course of more than 6000 years.

CAN WE GET IN CLOSE OR DO WE SETTLE FOR PHOTOS?

It's not possible to reach the peninsula by land, so local tours on a ferry are your only option, and these are subject to weather and water conditions. Don't let the logistics of the journey put you off, though; if the weather is on your side it's possible to rent a kayak and tour the caves under your own steam. The sight of the azure waters of the lake reflecting against the softly, psychedelic patterning of the caverns is worth all the trouble.

THERE ARE A FEW FORMATIONS IN OUR SIGHTS. WHICH ONE IS A 'MUST SEE'?

The three main marble sites are known as the Chapel, the Cathedral, and the Cave – don't miss the Cave. Its winding caverns, tunnels and towers are mesmerisingly lovely.

JUNEAU, ALASKA, USA

Mendenhall Ice Caves, Alaska, USA

WE NEVER IMAGINED IT WOULD BE POSSIBLE TO EXPLORE UNDERNEATH A GLACIER.

And the reality is even more beautiful than anything you can imagine. You need to be quick, however, if you'd like to experience this natural phenomenon first hand; global warming has caused the Mendenhall Glacier to begin retreating at an unsurpassed rate in the last 60 years. If we stay on this current path the ice caves will soon be gone.

OH NO! HURRY UP, LET'S GET IN AND HAVE A LOOK.

Fortune favours the brave, and in this case it also favours the persistent and the adventurous. To get in under the glacier you must first kayak across part of the Mendenhall Lake and then hike the West Glacier trail which takes you to the caves. An experienced guide will show you the way and also show you the path of least environmental impact.

THE REWARD LOOKS TO BE TOTALLY WORTH THE EFFORT.

It's not every day you can say you stood, completely encased in luminous blue ice, with the sights and sounds of glacial streams swirling and burbling around you.

NAPHAT CHANTARAVISOOT © GETTYIMAGES

44

50

The Mariana Trench, Western Pacific Ocean

CALL US CRAZY, BUT WE CAN'T SEE THERE BEING ANY TOURS TO THE TRENCH ANY TIME SOON.

True, the Mariana Trench doesn't see boatloads of tourists crowding the surface of the Pacific Ocean above the dark depths where the sea is at its deepest and most mysterious.

SO WHAT ARE WE DOING HERE IF WE CAN'T SEE ANYTHING?

It's hard to ignore the wondrous facts of this natural phenomenon. The trench is a staggering 2550km long and close to an average of 70km wide and at its deepest section, known as the Challenger Deep, it's 10,994m to the bottom. There has been an unrepeated depth measurement of 11,034m, but to all intents and purposes, it's just a bloody long way down.

IS THERE ANYTHING DOWN THERE APART FROM THE DARKNESS?

It's a veritable playground for microbial life and the single-celled Xenophyophores; amoebas that have been measured at a gigantic 10cm. In December 2014, a new species of snailfish was discovered at over 8000m below, making it the title-holder of the deepest living fish ever filmed.

Mountainous wonders

Huangguoshu Waterfall, China

THERE ARE THOUSANDS OF BEAUTIFUL WATERFALLS IN THE WORLD. WHAT IS IT ABOUT HUANGGUOSHU?

There are a few things that set this magnificent waterfall apart from countless others. First, it's one of the largest waterfalls in all of Asia, with a spectacular drop of nearly 80m; secondly, at over 100m wide, the amount of water flowing over the precipice creates a roar that can be heard for miles; and thirdly, the voluminous sheets of water from the Baishui River that plunge over the falls shelter a secret cave behind that can be accessed on foot.

WHO DOESN'T LOVE A SECRET CAVE?

Known as the imaginatively-named Water-Curtain Cave, the 13m-plus cavern is naturally formed and tucked neatly behind the raging waters. Proximity to the falls and their deafening noise is an exhilarating experience.

THIS DOESN'T LOOK TO BE THE ONLY WATERFALL IN THE HUANGGUOSHU NATIONAL PARK.

Although the park is named after its major drawcard, there are numerous other, smaller falls that are less dramatic but also less touristed, so equally fun to explore.

BIHAIBO © GETTY IMAGES

50

Lauterbrunnen Valley, Switzerland

IT'S HARD TO BELIEVE THIS PLACE HASN'T BEEN CREATED USING CGI.

With so many jaw-dropping sights in one frame, you couldn't make it up. We're here to guarantee that this is just what the Lauterbrunnen Valley looks like.

TALK US THROUGH ALL OF THE MAGNIFICENT NATURAL PHENOMENA WE CAN SEE.

There are over 72 waterfalls dotted throughout the valley, including the 30m-high Staubbach Falls, one of Europe's highest; there are also lush Alpine meadows; sheer cliff faces; dizzying mountain peaks; and several slow-moving glaciers.

IT'S SOUNDING LIKE AN EXTREME-SPORT-LOVER'S PARADISE.

It's certainly a choose-your-own-Alpine-adventure kind of place. You're spoilt for choice with skiing, mountaineering, rock-climbing, hiking, paragliding, mountain-biking, skydiving, or even dog-sledding all on the agenda.

JUST THE IDEA OF ALL THIS ACTIVITY IS MAKING US TIRED.

Then have a ride on one of the cable cars that travel between mountain peaks, or settle into a meadow picnic spot and just admire the view. There are many short walks close to valley villages that don't require an excess of adrenaline.

Milford Sound, South Island, New Zealand

NEW ZEALAND REALLY PUNCHES ABOVE ITS WEIGHT WHEN IT COMES TO NATURAL WONDERS, DOESN'T IT?

For a small country tucked away at the bottom of the earth there is a staggering bounty of nature's gifts on show. One of the most serenely lovely of these is Milford Sound.

THE WHOLE VISTA LOOKS SO WILD AND INACCESSIBLE.

Despite now being one of NZ's most visited tourist sites, the Fiordland region remained cut off to most of the world until a road to the Sound was finally opened in 1954. It still has a pristine and undiscovered feel (if you can see past the enormous cruise ships on the water) which is largely due to its inhospitable climate. Milford Sound is the wettest inhabited place in NZ and one of the wettest in the world.

THE RAIN IS PUTTING US OFF OUR HIKING AND CAMPING PLANS.

If the wet weather is putting a dampener on your outdoor activities, consider one of the famous boat cruises on the Sound. The boats can take you right up close to some of the spectacular waterfalls that crash for hundreds of metres over the edge of the surrounding sheer cliffs.

Mount Everest, Nepal and Tibet

THERE ARE NATURE'S WONDERS AND THEN THERE'S THE KING OF THE EARTH'S LANDSCAPE, MOUNT EVEREST.

Exactly: there are few natural wonders in the world that capture the imagination quite like Mount Everest, the planet's highest mountain at 8848m. This breathtaking behemoth is not a wonder to be approached lightly, however, as every year Everest claims the lives of some of the climbers attempting to scale its summit.

WHAT ABOUT IF WE JUST WANT TO GET TO BASE CAMP?

Even the mountain's two base camps (one on the south side in Nepal, and one on the north side in Tibet) are at altitudes of over 5000m. That's more than 200m higher than Mont Blanc – the highest peak in Europe. What we're trying to say is any attempt to get close to Everest is a serious pursuit, a once in a lifetime adventure.

OK, POINT TAKEN – GETTING TO KNOW EVEREST IS NOT FOR THE FAINT-HEARTED.

Don't let us put you off your quest. This is one of life's greatest challenges and brings its journey-makers the greatest reward. The epic proportions of an attempt on Everest are life-changing and if you make it you will join an exclusive club of humans who have come face to face with the true majesty of nature.

Mount Roraima, Gran Sabana, Venezuela

THAT IS ONE HEFTY WEDGE OF ROCK.
It's an awe-inspiring sight to see this enormous plateau of stone emerge from the mist. The top of the mountain marks the confluence of the borders of Venezuela, Brazil and Guyana, but is officially part of Venezuela's Canaima National Park. It is considered to be one of the oldest known geological formations in the world, dating from over two billion years ago.

THE SHEER CLIFF-SIDES OF THE MOUNTAIN MAKE IT LOOK LIKE WE WON'T BE GETTING TO THE TOP ANY TIME SOON.
All four sides do dramatically drop off over 400m to the forest floor below, making it a popular sight for only the serious, and very experienced, mountain climbers. That said, the mountain does have a section of its side that is less steep, where hikers can get to the summit after a walk of two days.

WE'RE SURE THE VIEW FROM UP HIGH IS WONDERFUL, BUT IT'S PRETTY SPECIAL TO BE ON THE GROUND TO SEE SOME OF THE WATERFALLS CASCADING OVER THE EDGES.
The cleanly carved away edges of the mountain and the almost daily rainfall on the summit's monolithic plateau combine to make for some extremely stunning waterfalls. Roraima Falls gushes over four tiers with a combined drop of over 600m.

Musandam Fjords, Oman

DID SOMEONE SAY THE 'NORWAY OF ARABIA'?

We can sort of see the similarities – minus the snow, of course. The fjords were formed over 20,000 years ago when polar ice caps melted and flooded the Musandam valleys. Now the deep inlets and bays are ringed by craggy peaks and steep cliffs creating Oman's most popular tourist attraction.

SNORKELLING IN A TURQUOISE SEA WAS NOT WHAT SPRANG TO MIND WHEN WE THOUGHT OF THE MIDDLE EAST.

A dhow cruise is the best way to start exploring this dramatic landscape. Aside from staring agog at the graphic white of the limestone surrounds, it's possible to snorkel in the calm and crystal-clear waters, and try to spot a dolphin or two.

APART FROM THE TOUR BOATS AND FISHING VESSELS, IT'S A PRETTY DESOLATE PLACE.

Here's a wacky bit of trivia for you about this isolated spot – in 1864, a telegraph station was built on what is now known as Telegraph Island. The station was designed to help lay an undersea cable from India to Basra and on to London; getting the cable 'around the bend' of the Persian Gulf gave rise to the expression, due to the difficulty of the job and the lonely and remote location of the fjord islands.

Perito Moreno Glacier, Argentina

SO THERE'S A FAIR CHOICE WHEN IT COMES TO THE WORLD'S MOST AMAZING GLACIERS... WHY THIS ONE?

A few stunning facts set Perito Moreno apart from other glaciers the world over. The first, most striking characteristic is that every four to five years the glacier advances enough to dam a part of the Argentino Lake, creating a massive rise in water levels, as much as 60m in some cases. The resulting pressure creates a rupture which sends enormous walls of ice crashing into Argentino Lake.

SOUNDS AMAZING BUT WHAT IF WE'RE NOT LUCKY ENOUGH TO BE THERE WHEN THE RUPTURE OCCURS? WILL WE STILL BE TREATED TO AN AWESOME SPECTACLE?

As one of only three glaciers worldwide that is actually growing rather than retreating, Perito Moreno ensures that anyone who makes the journey won't be disappointed. The glacier moves at a rate of almost two metres every day and when you're talking about an ice mass that is five kilometres wide and over 70m high, it's an impressive sight in anyone's books.

OK, WE'RE IMPRESSED.

Add to the glacier's modern-day drawcards the fact that it is one of the last surviving remnants of the last Ice Age (18,000 years ago) and you have a pretty cool experience all round.

MATT MUNRO © LONELY PLANET

The Grand Canyon, Arizona, USA

WE'VE ALL SEEN THE PHOTOS, DOES IT LIVE UP TO THE HYPE?

Photos schmotos: nothing can compare to visiting the Grand Canyon in person and seeing it in all its 'putting-into-perspective' grandeur. Close to 450km long and nearly 30km wide, the area cleaved by the Colorado River over the course of billions of years is rich in geological wonder and in Native American history.

CONSIDERING THE CANYON'S SIZE, WHERE'S THE BEST SPOT TO ENJOY THE VIEW?

The South Rim gives its steady stream of tourists a wonderful panoramic view of the winding way of the canyon and its layered lines of rock. But if you would like your sightseeing without the other travellers, we suggest a walk. Even just a short stroll from the major car parks will give you some breathing space. For the more adventurous, try the Kaibab Trail, which takes you down from the rim for a variation on the view.

AND FOR A GLIMPSE OF THE PEOPLE'S PAST?

Native American life is still present in the areas around, and in, the canyon. The Havasupai people are thought to have lived in the canyon for over 800 years and it's also known to be home to the Navajo and Hopi peoples. Look out for tours run by the descendants of these original inhabitants.

Tianzi Mountains, China

THESE ARE LIKE NO MOUNTAINS WE'VE EVER SEEN BEFORE.
The striking sandstone pillars that dominate this dramatic landscape are the result of millions of years of erosion. There are over 3000 vertical columns, each one festooned with densely growing pine trees that sprout for the sky, the highest of which is over 1250m tall. China honoured nature's handiwork in 1982 by naming the area in which the pillars stand the Zhangjiajie National Park, one of the country's first.

THE SCENERY LOOKS A LITTLE FAMILIAR.
Fans of one of the highest grossing films of all time, *Avatar*, will recognise the setting as the 'Hallelujah Mountains of Pandora'. Director James Cameron used images of the towering stone masts as inspiration for scenes in his record-breaking movie.

HOW DO WE GET UP CLOSE FOR THE BEST VIEW?
As if walking on wooden and rope platforms suspended hundreds of metres above sea level wasn't enough to cause a heart attack in anyone afraid of heights, the new thing is a truly terrifying glass-bottomed bridge that spans two cliffs in the Tianzi Mountains. The bridge is 430m long, six metres wide and gently sways above a 300m vertical drop.

Trolltunga, Norway

OH, NO WAY! THERE IS NO WAY WE'RE WALKING OUT ON THAT STONE PLANK.

Fair enough – this is not a mountain hike for anyone with even the vaguest hint of vertigo. The huge cantilevering slat of stone, known as the Troll Tongue, hovers 700m above the crystalline alpine waters of Lake Ringdalsvatnet, a total of 1100m above sea level. But if you're able to brave the dizzying heights, the payoff is sublime.

IT LOOKS SO INCREDIBLE WE'RE GOING TO GIVE IT A SHOT.

Be prepared. It's a long hike which takes around 10-12 hours (23km return) and ascends around 90m. It can also only be attempted in the summer months, as winter snow makes the route far too treacherous. For extra adventure, it's possible to camp in the mountainous area around Trolltunga.

CAMPING SOUNDS LIKE AN INGENIOUS WAY OF BREAKING UP THE HARD GRAFT.

It also means you can stay put for the spectacular sunset over the Folgefonna glacier and for the serene splendour of a sunrise, minus the day-tripping crowds.

Mystical and mythical

Aurora Borealis, Greenland

THIS IS ON MY BUCKET LIST.

It is, and on most other people's as well. Some people do it in Scandinavia, some in Alaska. But who can say they've been to Greenland? And it's one of the best places to see the sky light up with those fluorescent ribbons and swirls.

WHAT MAKES IT SO GOOD IN GREENLAND?

How about viewing it from a dogsled? That adds a certain charm, right? But practically speaking, Greenland is famed for clear skies, and clear skies means you're almost guaranteed a drenching in the cool green glow.

GUARANTEED, HUH?

Well, let's say if you're there between September and March, the odds are good. But a month either side of the season and you could still be in luck too.

AND APART FROM THE GREENLAND GLOW?

How about a Greenland floe? You could always incorporate a visit to the Jakobshavn Glacier – the likely source of the iceberg that sank the *Titanic*. And if your plans allow for it, legend has it that a child conceived beneath the play of these spectral visions will be a bright spark, so there's always that. Let the fireworks begin!

Fairy Pools, Isle of Skye, Scotland

FAIRIES, HEY?

If there's anywhere in the world that could convince you that these mythical creatures exist, this is it. Tucked into stunning highland scenery on the Scottish island of Skye, the site is a series of atmospheric pools, waterfalls and cascades, and small caves and caverns. Too pretty to be the haunt of mere humans.

WILL THE FAIRIES MIND IF WE TAKE A DIP?

The absolutely crystal clear waters are undeniably inviting: the water is so clean and pristine that you can see right to the moss-covered stones at the bottom of the pools. Be warned, though – the water is breathtakingly cold.

NO PROBLEM, WE'LL JUST JUMP BACK IN THE CAR AND HEAD BACK TO THE HOTEL.

As accommodating as the mountain pixies seem to be of visitors, they draw the line at motor vehicles. The only way in and out of the pools is by foot. It's a moderate 20-minute hike to the first waterfall – just enough time to work up a sweat.

50

Fingal's Cave, Staffa Island, Inner Hebrides, Scotland

WHO IS FINGAL AND WHY ARE WE GATECRASHING HIS CAVE?

The hero of an ancient Celtic legend, Fingal is the colossal Scottish rival of the Irish giant responsible for the Giant's Causeway in Northern Ireland (see page 78).

OH YEAH, WE CAN SEE THE SIMILARITIES.

They're part of the same natural phenomenon, an ancient lava flow that may have connected them over 60 million years ago.

THAT'S A MYSTICAL COMBINATION OF LEGEND AND FACT.

The remote and rare nature of the cave has captured the attention of famous Great Britons since its introduction to human consciousness by Sir Joseph Banks in 1772. There have been numerous poems, stories, songs and scores composed in its honour, and in Victorian times it became a must-see tourist site, attracting such luminaries as William Wordsworth, John Keats, Lord Tennyson and even Queen Victoria.

CAN WE STILL FOLLOW IN THESE FAMOUS FOOTSTEPS?

It's possible to hike to the cave over the uninhabited island of Staffa or board one of the boat cruises that take you close to the cave's entrance.

Giant's Causeway, County Antrim, Northern Ireland

IT'S HARD TO BELIEVE THAT THIS BIZARRE GEOMETRICALLY-STRUCTURED SITE HAS BEEN FORMED AU NATUREL.

You're not the only ones to have trouble believing that the interlocking basalt columns are the result of an ancient volcanic eruption. Pfft, yeah right. It's much more likely that these extraordinary stone structures were carved into a causeway by an enormous giant who wanted to use the stepping stones to cross the North Channel to Scotland in order to take up the challenge to fight from his equally gigantic Scottish counterpart. There are identical basalt columns over the sea, at Fingal's Cave on the isle of Staffa in Scotland (see page 76).

AND IT'S POSSIBLE FOR US ORDINARY HUMAN FOLK TO FOLLOW IN THE FOOTSTEPS OF THE GIANT?

Mere mortals just need to walk for 800m from the visitor centre to hop over the hexagonal columns to their heart's content. Keep in mind, however, that the causeway ranks as one of the top tourist spots in the whole United Kingdom so you may well be dealing with giant crowds as well as the giant's handiwork.

ANY TIPS FOR EXPERIENCING THE CAUSEWAY WITHOUT THE CROWDS?

Try walking along the cliff-side above the causeway for spectator-free, spectacular views.

The Waitomo Glow-worm Caves, North Island, New Zealand

GLOW-WORMS – CUTE.

Touring the limestone caves illuminated with the phosphorescence of thousands upon thousands of tiny glow-worms sure is an other-worldly experience. Made up of three different levels the last level, known as the Cathedral, is where you board a boat on the Waitomo River to drift underground through the Glow-worm Grotto. It is most serenely beautiful. The only light comes from the worms that twinkle and shine on the roof of the cave.

AND WHAT OF THE OTHER LEVELS OF THE CAVES WITHOUT THE WORMS?

Stunningly lit to make the most of the spectacular stalactite and stalagmite formations, the cave's other chambers are equally striking places to explore.

DON'T GET US WRONG, THIS ALL SOUNDS VERY NICE... BUT WHAT IF WE'RE AFTER SOME ADVENTURE?

For the daring among you, the veritable plethora of small caverns and tunnels carved by underground streams can be explored by blackwater rafting or by zip-lining and abseiling through the lesser-known spaces. If you choose rafting you'll be issued with your own rubber tube for floating through the wetter areas, but be prepared to crawl and wade in parts where the caves get very narrow.

50

Uluru, Northern Territory, Australia

IS THERE ANY MORE ICONIC NATURAL WONDER IN AUSTRALIA?

In a nation not short of natural wonders, the immense spectacle that awaits you in Australia's vast red centre is truly breathtaking. The solitary grandeur of the rock is worthy of every superlative you can think to throw at it; and even then no description can really prepare you for the sight of over 3.5km of solid stone in real life.

WE KNOW ULURU HAS IMPORTANT SPIRITUAL SIGNIFICANCE FOR ABORIGINAL PEOPLE.

The Pitjantjatjara tribe have called the area home for many thousands of years and there are many sacred sites around the base of the rock that have deep cultural and spiritual meaning. Learn more about the Dreamtime legends surrounding the rock at the Uluru-Kata Tjuta Aboriginal Cultural Centre, and take a tour of ancient cave paintings with Aboriginal guides.

WE KNOW NOT TO CLIMB ULURU, SO WHAT'S THE BEST WAY TO TAKE IT ALL IN?

Sunrise and sunset are when the rock turns on the most spectacular show. From bright orange to ochre to deep browns and black, it's a constantly changing lightshow that draws gasps of wonder from the mesmerised crowds.

National parks

Kakadu National Park, Northern Territory, Australia

THIS WOULD HAVE TO QUALIFY AS THE MIDDLE OF NOWHERE, YES?

The effort to get here might be epic, but the rewards are just as magnificent. Most people access Kakadu from the Northern Territory's small but vibrant state capital, Darwin, a lazy 4000km drive from Sydney. From Darwin, it's another 250km to the park itself.

AND OUR JOURNEY'S REWARD?

A 20,000sq km-sized slice of one of the earth's most geologically dramatic and biologically diverse wildernesses. The park supports four major river systems; has six different landforms, including estuaries, floodplains, stone country and the southern hills. There are over 280 different bird species, around 60 species of mammals, more than 10,000 insect species, and lots and lots of crocodiles. DO NOT go swimming.

SUCH A SUPERB SETTING MUST HAVE SIGNIFICANCE TO THE TRADITIONAL OWNERS OF THE LAND?

It is believed that Aboriginal people have inhabited the Kakadu region for more than 40,000 years, forging a deeply spiritual relationship with the region. There are more than 5000 Aboriginal art sites throughout the park, with some hosting rock art paintings over 20,000 years old, one of the longest historical records of any people in the world.

MARANHAO, BRAZIL

Lencois Maranhenses National Park, Maranhao, Brazil

WE HAD VISIONS OF BRAZIL'S NATURAL WONDERS BEING ALL FORESTS AND JUNGLES, NOT THIS EXPANSE OF SAND.
Being one of the largest countries on earth, Brazil supports a surprising variety of ecological phenomena, the sand dunes of Lencois Maranhenses being one of the most unexpected and astounding.

HOW ON EARTH DID ALL THAT WATER GET IN BETWEEN ALL THE DUNES?
The park has two river systems running through it which gently push sand from the interior of the park towards the Atlantic Ocean. In the dry season, strong winds push the sand back inland to form sculpted dunes. From January to June the park gets pelted with heavy rain which pools in the valleys of the dunes, creating the spectacle that earned the park its reputation.

WITH THE DUNES SEEMINGLY AT THE MERCY OF THE SEASONS, IS THERE A BEST TIME TO VISIT?
The lagoons of water are only in existence for a couple of months a year and are at their most spectacular in July, just after the heaviest of the rains. In this month many aquamarine pools are over 300ft long and more than 10ft deep.

RUDI SEBASTIAN © GETTYIMAGES

50

Plitvice Lakes National Park, Croatia

WHAT A PRETTY SIGHT.

Nature sure knows how to turn on a good show, doesn't she? This series of 16 terraced lakes with sparkling clear water cascading over from one to another is picturesquely situated among the trees in the vast forest of Croatia's largest national park. Nature's bounty has been framed for human use by the sympathetic use of wooden walkways and footbridges.

THAT SOUNDS LIKE A VERY CIVILISED WAY TO HIKE.

It's easy to see why this is one of Europe's most popular natural wonders – it's possible to follow the walkways around the edges of the crystalline pools, over sections of the gushing water, and even right behind and underneath some of the waterfalls.

WHAT ABOUT GOING IN FOR A DIP?

Around, under and over, but not in. Swimming is prohibited, but you can jump on one of the park's free boats for a different perspective on the lakes and waterfalls. The boats head from high to low, beginning at Kozjak, the largest of the lakes at around four kilometres in length. Don't miss the Veliki Slap, the tallest waterfall in Croatia at 78m.

KELLY CHENG © GETTY IMAGES/FLICKR RF

The Wildebeest Migration, Serengeti to Masai Mara, Africa

THIS LOOKS LIKE A NATURAL WONDER WE DON'T WANT TO GET TOO CLOSE TO.

From near or far, this, the world's biggest migration of animals, is an annual event on a massive scale. Over two million beasts make their way from the Serengeti to the green grass of the Masai Mara. Fear of missing out means that zebras, gazelles, and impalas also join the wildebeest in their frantic journey towards a good feed.

WHERE'S THE BEST PLACE TO GET A GOOD LOOK AT THE STAMPEDE?

Watching the herds cross the Mara River in the northern Serengeti is high drama. The animals frantically fight the gushing waters to get from one side to the other; crocodiles on the look-out for an easy meal make the crossing even more high stakes.

AND ONCE THEY REACH THE GREENER GRASS ON OTHER SIDE?

It doesn't take long for the animals to gorge themselves on the smorgasbord of fresh grass on the Masai Mara and once the dinner plains are empty, they all turn around and head back to where they came from.

WWW.NPS.GOV/YOSE

Yosemite National Park, California, USA

THERE'S PLENTY OF NATURAL WONDERS TO CHOOSE FROM IN AMERICA; WHY YOSEMITE?
Yosemite National Park is like a Greatest Hits album, no other national park in the United States delivers more bang for your buck. From giant sequoia groves to soaring granite cliffs, and gorgeous mountain lakes to slowly advancing glaciers, every corner of this 750,000-acre park is nature at its best.

WITH SO MANY SPECTACULAR SIGHTS, WHERE DO WE START?
A majority of the nearly four million annual visitors to the park spend their time in the Yosemite Valley. This glacial valley is 13km long and surrounded by the park's big hitters, including the stunning granite peaks of El Capitan and Half Dome. The Merced River flows through the valley feeding smaller creeks, including the Yosemite Creek, which eventually plunges over the Yosemite Falls, the highest waterfall in North America.

WITH SO MANY VISITORS TO THE VALLEY, ARE WE GOING TO BE ON A TOURIST CONVEYER BELT PAST MAJOR SIGHTS?
The sheer number of walking and hiking trails in the valley means you can always find some solitude amongst the majesty. To ensure you have a patch of the park to yourself, try hiking one of the trailheads that takes you out of the valley and away from the crowds.

Strange landscapes

Bristlecone Pines, California, USA

EXCUSE OUR SCEPTICISM, BUT IT'S HARD TO BELIEVE A PINE TREE WILL BLOW OUR MINDS.

There are a few special characteristics that the Bristlecones have up their spikey sleeves that set them apart from their flora friends, such as that they're believed to be some of the oldest living organisms in the world. The eldest, 'Mesthuselah', is nearly 4850 years old. That's nearly 2500 years older than the Acropolis in Greece, for some perspective.

WHAT ELSE IS SO WONDERFUL ABOUT THESE GNARLY-LOOKING THINGS?

The twisted trunks and branches on these squat seniors are decorated with beautiful swirling patterns of greys and browns; and, despite some greenery at the end of some of the branches, the tree looks almost devoid of life, which makes for a dramatic stance, especially when contrasted against the rocky outcrops of the White Mountains.

CAN YOU POINT OUT 'MESTHUSELAH'? WE'D LIKE TO TAKE A CLOSER LOOK.

Scientists studying the trees won't let on which ones are the oldest after a 4862-year-old tree was cut down in 1964 by a geologist looking for evidence of Ice Age glaciers.

Crooked Forest, Poland

SOMETIMES IT LOOKS LIKE THE EARTH IS HAVING US ON.
So far no one has figured out how these quirky kinked trees in a pine forest in northwest Poland came to be.

ARE THERE ANY THEORIES?
The 400-tree strong forest is approximately 85 years old; and that's where our information pool runs dry. Planted just before the start of the Second World War, there is a theory that the trunks were deliberately kinked in their infancy in order to be used for boat-building or furniture making, but after the occupation of Poland by Nazi forces the forest was abandoned. Another theory speculates that the pines were knocked to the side by a severe snowstorm. Nobody really knows.

WE'LL GO WITH NATURE'S SENSE OF HUMOUR.
The mystery of the forest's origin just adds to its otherworldly charm. There's no denying this peculiar place has a strange and magical attraction, like a picturesque scene from a fairy tale.

SAHARA DESERT, MAURITANIA

Eye of the Sahara, Mauritania

THERE'S A SUPERNATURAL SOUND TO THIS NATURAL WONDER.

Like a sandy crop circle in the middle of the desert, this mysterious disc sticks out like a sore thumb amongst miles of featureless sand. It is in such start contrast to its surrounds that it can clearly be seen from space and was once thought to be the result of a gigantic meteor strike.

SCIENCE IS ABOUT TO DEBUNK ALL THE MYTHS NOW, ISN'T IT?

Of course! Instead of an enormous asteroid crashing into the earth's surface, it's now believed that the site is a significantly eroded and amazingly symmetrical geological dome. The concentric circles are layers of alternating rock; sedimentary, metamorphic, and igneous. The sedimentary rock in the centre of the ring is thought to be 2.5 billion years old. How's that for some serious science?

CAN WE SEE ANY OF THIS FROM GROUND LEVEL?

To be honest, the earth really made this wonder to be viewed from above, so it will be something nice to look at when we all move to the moon.

Ice Towers of Mount Erebus, Antarctica

TRAVELLING TO THE END OF THE EARTH TO SEE AN ACTIVE VOLCANO BUBBLING THROUGH THE ICE? WE MIGHT HAVE TO TAKE YOUR WORD FOR THIS ONE.

It's true the astounding ice towers of the volcanically active Mount Erebus are not part of a well-trodden tourist trail, so let us talk you through their wondrous properties. The ice towers are formed when warm volcanic gases escape through caverns in the ice creating a chimney-like structure with the toxic gas flowing out the top. There are hundreds of these towers on the mountain's slopes and at heights of nearly 20m, it makes for a dramatic and surreal sight.

WE COULD BE ON A DIFFERENT PLANET – NOT ONE THAT SUPPORTS HUMAN LIFE.

Add to the inhospitable temperatures and wild, barren landscape the fact that the volcano is continuously bubbling and spewing huge hunks of molten rock through the air and you'll be happy to call any landform north of Antarctica home.

SAYING THAT, THERE ARE OBVIOUSLY SOME BRAVE SOULS FACING THE MOUNTAIN'S WRATH.

Since its discovery in 1841 Erebus has been a magnet for explorers and scientists, keen to experience the volcano in all its glory.

Living Root Bridges of Cherrapunji, Meghalaya, India

THIS SOUNDS LIKE SOMETHING OUT OF *LORD OF THE RINGS.*

The twisted, gnarly root systems that stretch and grow across the fast-flowing rivers in far north-eastern India look indeed like the stuff of fantasy.

HOW HAS THIS COME TO BE?

The trees are a particular species of rubber tree with extraordinarily strong root systems that thrive in the hot and humid climate. The trees are also able to grow a secondary system of roots from the middle of their trunks, which warp and weave over and around their surroundings.

AND TO GET ACROSS THE WATER?

Here's where the roots get a little help from their human friends. Local tribespeople recognised the potential and strength of the tree roots in being able to assist them in crossing the many raging rivers so they devised a plan to support the rubber roots with straight branches, enabling them to grow in a direct line across the water; once on the other side the rubber roots take hold.

HOW STURDY CAN THESE THINGS BE?

Many of the bridges have taken decades to grow and are so strong they're able to support the weight of 50 people at once. Because they are living structures, the bridges actually get stronger with age.

50

Pamukkale, Turkey

THIS IS NO OFF-THE-BEATEN-TRACK NATIONAL TREASURE, IF THE TOURIST HOARDS ARE ANYTHING TO GO BY.
That's true, this dramatic stack of blindingly white travertine terraces is Turkey's number one tourist drawcard. But don't let that put you off. And here's a tip: stay overnight near the terraces and visit first thing in the morning before the busloads begin arriving.

RIGHT, WE KNOW ALL ABOUT THE TOURISTS, TELL US MORE ABOUT THE NATURAL WONDER.
The terraces are formed by the build-up of carbonate mineral from the warm water flowing from the thermal springs above. Pools form at the edge of the terraces where people have bathed for thousands of years.

DID YOU SAY 'THOUSANDS OF YEARS?'
We did. Ancient Greco-Romans built the city of Hierapolis on the site of the mineral springs in order to soak up the perceived health benefits of the warm spring water. These days the crumbled ruins of this ancient city can be seen at the bottom of some of the pools. The combination of these man-made wonders and nature's beauty is the reason you'll be sharing the site with so many friends.

Sagano Bamboo Forest, Japan

IT'S LIKE BEING TRANSPORTED TO AN ALTERNATIVE REALITY.

The rows and rows of softly swaying bamboo stalks rise metres into the sky to almost touch at their tips, creating a canopy and the sense of being inside a green room. It's a dreamy feeling and if it were possible to escape the noises of your fellow travellers chatting and posing for selfies you would be able to hear a sound that has been classified by the Japanese Ministry of the Environment as one of the '100 Soundscapes of Japan'.

CAN YOU DESCRIBE THESE SOUNDS?

It's the combination of gentle breezes rustling the leaves and the thin wooden trunks of the bamboo stalks creaking and knocking together. A sound designated to be quintessentially Japanese in its meditative and calming nature.

THE CROWDS OF TOURISTS LOOK LIKE THEY'RE THREATENING THE SERENITY.

Sorry about that – it's probably books like this one that helped to create the crush of people desperate to witness the spectacle in their lifetime. If it all gets too crazy, remember to look up. There are no smartphones in the treetops.

ABDERAZAK TISSOUKAI © 500PX

Salar de Uyuni, Bolivia

I CAN FEEL A THIRST COMING ON.
Ten billion tonnes of salt can do that to you. But you're not here to have fish and chips, you're here to see the largest salt flat on the planet, one of the flattest places on earth. It almost defies description.

GIVE IT A GO.
Anything for you. Well, in dry times it's the parched, cracked surface of caked salt, hard and brittle. The salt layer can be metres thick – how amazing is that?! And the expression 'flat as a tack'? It was actually invented to describe this place.

NO WAY!
Ok, maybe not true exactly. But seriously, it's so flat you can see forever.

YOU SOUND DELIRIOUS.
Back to the description. It's most incredible when January rains have left the expanse as a giant mirror. You need to go, and you need to look at the real thing, but Google Image this place – the reflections create the kind of shots that burn into your memory. If this place doesn't have you agog with wonder, nowhere will. Oh, and pink flamingos. Don't miss the pink flamingos. They will be the icing on the cake.

Socotra Island and Archipelago, Indian Ocean, Yemen

LOOKS LIKE MOTHER NATURE HAS HAD SOME WILLY WONKA-LIKE FUN ON THIS ISLAND.

Isolated at sea, more than 300km from Yemen and approximately 250km from Somalia, the Socotra Archipelago has gone ahead and created its own unique set of flora and fauna adapted to its harsh and unforgiving environment.

OK, YOU'RE GOING TO HAVE TO TALK US THROUGH WHAT WE'RE LOOKING AT HERE.

One of the most interesting and bizarre looking specimens on Socotra Island is the dramatically-named Dragon Blood Tree. From a distance it looks like a giant, long-stemmed mushroom, but up close you can see the intricate web of thin branches that jostle together to push their green leaves towards the sun, creating the flying saucer-like shape. The name comes from the red resin that oozes from the branches if they're cut.

DOES THIS DRY AND ROCKY LANDSCAPE SUPPORT ANIMAL LIFE?

There are over 140 species of birds, 10 of which can only be found in this remote corner of the world. There is one native mammal, a bat; and numerous reptiles, like skinks, lizards, and chameleons. Oh, and around 40,000 humans call the islands home.

MARIO EDER © GETTYIMAGES

OSOYOOS, BRITISH COLUMBIA, CANADA

Spotted Lake, British Columbia, Canada

THAT CANNOT POSSIBLY BE NATURAL.
Laid out like an enormous game of Twister, the colourful spots are actually mineral deposits left behind when a majority of the water evaporates from the lake during the warm summer months.

WHY ALL THE DIFFERENT COLOURS?
The various colours are brought out by the variation in the kind of mineral composition and due to the amount of rain the lake has received. The largest mineral deposits are those of magnesium sulphate, calcium, and sodium sulphates.

CAN WE GET UP CLOSE FOR A LOOK?
The Syilx people, the indigenous custodians of the land in which Spotted Lake is situated, have revered the area as a sacred site for hundreds of years. They believe that the waters have medicinal and therapeutic properties and so protect the area as an important cultural site and as an ecologically sensitive place. That said, it's still possible to pull up to the fence and get a decent view of this strange dotted space.

FARAFRA, EGYPT

White Desert, Egypt

WHERE ARE WE? EGYPT OR THE MOON?

This surreal lunar-like landscape is the result of hundreds of years of erosion coupled with wild, white-sandstorms that carve out crazy looking statues made from calcium rock.

IS IT JUST ME, OR DO SOME OF THEM LOOK LIKE RECOGNISABLE OBJECTS?

As trippy as it may seem to see a chalk statue shaped like an ice-cream cone or perhaps a mushroom, take heart, you're not the first. Many of the structures have actually been given names that reflect their oddly familiar shape. See if you can spot the chicken and tree (also known as the chicken and atomic bomb).

IT'S A BLINDINGLY BEAUTIFUL SIGHT DESPITE THE DAYTIME HEAT.

If the desert sun sounds like it will be too much to bear then consider joining a tour led by Bedouin guides where you camp overnight in the calcium basin. The rich red and orange hues from the setting sun create a magnificent display when they move over the sculptural shapes.

About the author

Kalya Ryan is in constant awe of nature's beauty and grandeur and could gaze for days at cloud-piercing mountain peaks, jaw-dropping waterfalls, prehistoric glaciers, vast sandy deserts, and deserted tropical beaches, but until she receives that longed-for lottery win she settles for quiet bushwalks in Victorian forests.

Index

Africa

Antarctica

FRANCESCO RICCA IACOMINO © GETTY IMAGES

Asia

Europe

North America

Oceania

South America

Other

More things to blow your mind

50 Bars to Blow Your Mind

Lonely Planet handpicks the world's most extraordinary drinking holes, from caverns and island party havens to a bar nestled in an ancient tree trunk.
ISBN 978-1-76034-058-2

50 Museums to Blow Your Mind

Whether you're a history buff, tech-head or have an inexplicable fascination with clowns, you'll find world-class collections here to pique your interest.
ISBN 978-1-76034-060-5

50 Beaches to Blow Your Mind

Discover the planet's most pristine, jaw-dropping, wild and wonderful sandy spots.

ISBN 978-1-76034-059-9

50 Places to Stay to Blow Your Mind

With these extraordinary offerings around the world, even sleeping will be an adventure on your next trip.
ISBN 978-1-78657-405-3

50 Festivals to Blow Your Mind

Whatever you like to celebrate, you'll find a gathering somewhere on the planet to suit you. Find the greatest festivals for you to set your sights on.
ISBN 978-1-78657-404-6

Published in May 2017 by Lonely Planet
Global Limited, CRN 554153
www.lonelyplanet.com
ISBN 978 1 78657 406 0
© Lonely Planet 2017
Printed in China
10 9 8 7 6 5 4 3 2 1

Written by **Kalya Ryan**
Managing Director, Publishing **Piers Pickard**
Associate Publisher **Robin Barton**
Commissioning Editor **Jessica Cole**
Art Direction **Daniel Di Paolo**
Layout Designer **Austin Taylor**
Editor **Kate Turvey**
Picture Researcher **Christina Webb**
Print Production **Larissa Frost, Nigel Longuet**
Cover image **Bryce Canyon, USA © Brad
McGinley Photography / Getty Images**

Lonely Planet offices

STAY IN TOUCH lonelyplanet.com/contact

AUSTRALIA The Malt Store, Level 3, 551
Swanston St, Carlton, Victoria 3053
03 8379 8000

IRELAND Unit E, Digital Court, The Digital
Hub, Rainsford St, Dublin 8

USA 124 Linden St, Oakland, CA 94607,
510 250 6400

UNITED KINGDOM 240 Blackfriars Rd,
London SE1 8NW, 020 3771 5100

Although the authors and Lonely Planet have
taken all reasonable care in preparing this
book, we make no warranty about the accuracy
or completeness of its content and, to the
maximum extent permitted, disclaim all liability
from its use.

Paper in this book is certified against the Forest
Stewardship Council™ standards. FSC™ promotes
environmentally responsible, socially beneficial and
economically viable management of the world's forests.

July 17